EYE AGAINST EYE

OTHER BOOKS BY FORREST GANDER

POETRY

Sound of Summer Running
(photographs by Ray Meeks)

12 x Twelve
(art by Tjibbe Hooghiemstra)

The Blue Rock Collection
(drawings by Rikki Ducornet)

Torn Awake

Science & Steepleflower

Deeds of Utmost Kindness

Lynchburg

Rush to the Lake

TRANSLATIONS

The Night: A Poem by Jaime Saenz
(with Kent Johnson)

No Shelter: Selected Poems by Pura López Colomé

Immanent Visitor: Selected Poems by Jaime Saenz
(with Kent Johnson)

Mouth to Mouth: Poems by Twelve Contemporary Mexican Women

Of Their Ornate Eyes of Crystalline Sand: Poems by Coral Bracho

ESSAYS

A Faithful Existence: Reading, Memory and Transcendence

FORREST GANDER

EYE AGAINST EYE

With Ten Photographs by
SALLY MANN

A NEW DIRECTIONS BOOK

Photographs in "Late Summer Entry: the Landscapes of Sally Mann," used by kind permission of Sally Mann.

Book design by Sylvia Frezzolini Severance
Manufactured in the United States of America
New Directions Books are printed on acid-free paper.
First published as a New Directions Paperbook Original (NDP1026) in 2005.
Published simultaneously in Canada by Penguin Books Canada Limited.

Library of Congress Cataloging-in-Publication Data

Gander, Forrest, 1956-
Eye against eye / Forrest Gander ; with ten photographs by Sally Mann.
    p. cm.
"New Directions paperbook original."
ISBN 0-8112-1635-7 (acid-free paper)
I. Title.
PS3557.A47E97 2005
811'.54—dc22
                                        2005014907

New Directions Books are published for James Laughlin
by New Directions Publishing Corporation
80 Eighth Avenue, New York, 10011

For Mike Perrow and Lida Junghaus,
and for the flicker outside my window

ACKNOWLEDGMENTS

"Late Summer Entry: the Landscapes of Sally Mann" was first published in two issues of *Conjunctions:* issue 32, 1999, and issue 37, 2001.

"Present Tense" was published in *Crowd,* Spring 2005.

"Mission Thief" was published in *Conjunctions,* Spring 2005.

"Ligature 1" and "Ligature 3" were commissioned by Sam Truitt and featured, with the sculpture of Douglas Culhane, in the exhibition *Magnitude: Words in Sculpture,* Rubenstein Gallery, New York, NY, 2001. They were first published in *First Intensity* (2002).

"Burning Tower, Standing Wall" was first published in *The Blue Rock Collection* (Salt Editions, 2004-05).

TABLE OF CONTENTS

Poem   1

Burning Towers, Standing Wall   3

Ligature   19

Present Tense   21

Ligature 2   35

Late Summer Entry: the Landscapes of Sally Mann   37

Ligature 3   61

Mission Thief   63

Ligature 4   79

EYE AGAINST EYE

Poem

Some
we say we
know go
like a window
dark.
Pathetic
any remark
then.
They leave
us, what
we call
them.

BURNING TOWERS, STANDING WALL

Burning Towers, Standing Wall

(Tabasco Province, Mexico)

I.

At sunset the surface of the wall gleams gold gleaming
and seems from even a short distance a smooth
impenetrable force swelling forward to meet the light
or the gaze of the visitor to the Maya ruin and locals
offer their service as guides or show what they mean
to sell in a mixed language of numbers and night
disperses everyone but insects crawling into fissures
in the crumble, field stones and mortar and flat
stacking stones, which divide *what* from *what once*

So doves come, a spotted turkey, iguana and
lately a pair of trogons to sit like lords on the ruin
where rocks flake away in rain and birdshit
in which seeds set, shell-stripped in the bellies
of the birds or wind-sown, sending up
stem and aigrette into unkind light and wind
while colorless thread-thin roots
force cracks in the capstones
to give way, rain and sunbake
dissolving mafic bonds as the exposure
vesicles inward

Some of the sounds bouncing from the stones are
nearly the same sounds *they* heard—resonant
human voices and the perwicka perwicka
of a quetzal in flight at a distance—
and give us access to them almost
through grinding cicadas and crickets
thrumming serrated thighs
though their domestic acoustics, the high
rubato laugh of children and the basso
continuo of city commotion
have precipitated out
leaving a gravitas around the ruin and into this
the walls swell with oxidation
and orange lichens press outward,
the crust flakes off into rain
and termite clatter, the chimmuck of falling pebbles,
undertones the stones conduct
along cleavage planes
so that if decibels diminish
as they approach silence
but never entirely fade,
this fresh patter is stirred into a vibrating, immeasurably
thin memorial ache inside the walls
and as primordial

II.

What came over the walls was drought, the 206-year
cyclical brightening of the sun, umber dust from the fields lifted
and blew into joints between stones, the pocks in the stones,
boys running along the god-faced wall
wiped their fingers on an altar
freshly carved from soft green
trachyte already hardening, exposed to air,
into a delicate grey,
fewer and fewer hand marks,
the number of shadows across the stones dwindling,
the same number of walls, resilient limestone blocks quarried
with a basalt axe, wood pry, bound together
with mud-gravel and lime cement,
plastered on the stones with trowels
and fingers, the crisp imprint of a fir needle
from a thousand years ago visible
in the desiccated mortar

What came over the walls was the enemy the conquered ones
the immiserated poor the infidels who
scaled stones on the knotted rope of their alien language
on spikes of vengeance with fire this section of the wall
shivered then and this part split like a lip, thatch and wooden lintels
burned as the enemy climbed through
the pitch and rhythm of their shouting rebounded from the stones
and screams clotted-off in smoke that veiled the city and
licked into those meticulous slits that represent
the iris of the human eye in figures
stuccoed to the collapsing temple's roof

What came over the wall was disease a plague

the priests could not avert a plague that made the stone

builders distrust each other and steal away

from walls they laid in a square clearing on the

scarp of a mountain and plague followed them

into the wilderness with a yowl

like a clay saucer making circles on the floor,

and though, as ever, cumulonimbus

pompadoured over the far mountains,

crows swirled above

the abandoned pyramid and king vultures

drove them off and even sea birds flew in and

squawked from the walls in hordes

ransacking corpses for their flesh and the stones

were white-crested and dribbled argent bird-lime

The Spaniards blew up the walls to see

behind them blasted the walls and crushed them

to pave roads to extinguish the trace the refuge

of the heathen to make noise they

mutilated stelae rubbed out glyphs the bark

codices burned and the temple frieze behind the stelae,

and to traces of blood and resin in braziers and on

altar stones they sluiced fresh blood, they chipped away

a relief carving in pumice of the former

ruler holding a manikin scepter, the facing stones

squared, well-smoothed and fitted

toppled into a monolithic mass of rubble and

mortar no girder still itself among

What lifts over the wall are gnats, iridescent butterflies,

a haze of mosquitoes, the night carousing

click-songs of wukus or cacomixtles

rummaging through the showy blossoms

of a Capparis tree whose trunk and roots

hold back the rubbish of the wall where it breached,

some animal that leaves relicts of katydids in its feces

comes over the wall,

and the scent of nectar comes over the wall,

the anniversaries of eyes.

III.

One over two, two over one. You must look
until you find the flat side of a round stone.
Don't put the largest on the bottom, but assemble
a communion. They rise to the surface of fields
in the rainy season.

One over two, two over one. Shim the round
stone with the flat. Lay a cross-stone here
to bind thicknesses. After you harvest
sandstone, use a chert wedge to bevel a fissure
where you want it to break. One
over two, stagger the joints.

Two over one, one over two. This stone weighs
three arrobas and no man could lift it. We are given
to understand that by means of a special whistle
the stones, big as they are,
arranged themselves
without any help to form these walls
for the first upright people.

Position the flatter side upward. Mix the crushed
and burnt limestone in a calcite bowl to render
sticky plaster. Start at the bottom, work across,
and then move up a row. Larger cap stones
stabilize the walls. One over two, two over one.

An index finger dressing a joint will
fix in the mortar its mark, an intimacy
to surpass every other gesture the hand
has made. What went on
behind these walls and who stood here
and hissed out or was massacred
so that our imagination of them is saturated
with encounter? And what do they frame
if not the intuition of our relation,
a resonance? They who heard also
the echo of hammers and dogs upwelling
into their hills. And followed Venus with their eyes
on its transverse. And stood near this same wall
noting the caliber and flow of a stream of urine.
Two stones butted together in a course and another
stone laid over the seam. Who sopped-in
laughter and met pain with breath. And sank under
the ceaselessly breaking wave of event, *is*
conjugating *here.* The fragility of presence. A bird
perched at the tip of a branch. Singing, we say.

Ligature

When the strong drag of the boy's adolescence pulls through them, the family rises into thinness and begins to break like a wave.

You turned away when I kissed you, the woman says. Why?

Half-lidded days of early winter.

When he points toward the woman, the boy looks at his hand the way dogs will.

The boy's jaw sets. As though behind his teeth, into the soft flesh of his throat, a new set of teeth were cutting through. A mouth for what?

Each of them adopts a private view. Arguments veer every which way, and who can follow? A sequence of dark non sequiturs blows in.

When one, when one word, when the word suicide enters the room where they are shouting, the system closes down, prematurely becalmed.

The man writes, I am not given a subject but am given to my subject. I am inside it like a parasite.

He sees the woman's face contract at the approach of other futures than the one for which her face was prepared.

So they inhabit their bodies like music, for a given time. And yet he continues to act as if there were times to come.

I just want you to go away, one of them screams.

Expressionless and flat as a tortilla, the afternoon moon over their house.

She calls the man to a corner in the basement. Those aren't spider eggs, he says, backing up. Those are its eyes.

When the encounter with the self is volcanic, nothing can follow.

Tearing open the cocoon to reveal itself, a boy within the family.

As if they were waiting. As if inside experience, bright with meaning, there were another experience pendant, unnameable.

PRESENT TENSE

Present Tense

In an epoch dominated by stars some speak softly into wafer phones

some milk caged bears for bile

for some the silhouette of a thronged city

flickers beneath a flickering sky

the gods squeeze themselves into icons for some

the hum of cables under the street

men in Zegna suits whose fathers entering theaters

tucked their cuffs into their socks

as a prophylactic against rats

white and hippopotamine tourists take to the beach

particles in solar wind carry field lines of the sun's magnetic force

into the penetralia of the solar system

As if nothing were wrong egrets dip-feed in near shore channels

the human genome reveals chromosomes from parasites

annexed by our DNA long ago

mongrels to the core and tourists

with cameras take the front pews

the enemy blows himself up at Passover dinner

the enemy trembles in a cave starving

the enemy lets go a daisy cutter

a million cubic feet of mud slides down the slope

toward a single bungalow in Laguna Beach

This is going to be a fast trip

alligator-cracks in the macadam and

fist-sized chunks of road torn out by wind

grey-black backs and bulbous snouts of northern right whales

cut the swell beyond Fire Island

each repeating sun a comet

world of physical event and mind's world indissoluble

but who will thrust a hand in to find the *mo-lo*

the veins and arteries of it

a sobering enthusiasm for the unmoored

no longer defining narrative

By mid-morning thrushes go quiet

in fingerling birches the hay field

exhales two tons of water

and someone who leaped into your life

like a crown fire blows out

in an ambulance trailing its hee-haw siren

insects called death watches

click behind the wall what happens

to the virtuosity of feeling as it meets

the mineral-hard quiddity of the world

while half a continent of raptors

funnels into the narrow

corridor along Lake Ontario's edge

or sweeps through the gash of Lake Champlain Valley

toward Mount Defiance

with your depression like a retinue of black centipedes

was how you left Arkansas

Leaving the pervasive aroma of sweet fern for rainwater

clotted with motor oil, dog feces, brake-lining residue

gushing from manholes into streets overrunning

the treatment plant spilling into Narragansett Bay

to poison quahogs and little-necks

where mild days and cold nights compound pressure

between the outer bark and dead heartwood

as maple sap drips out through spiles

you whose father crisscrossed the Mississippi

selling miraculous cures for cancer

the complaint of which he died

your mother's voice remembered as a subsong

a subdued warbling of vague intention

far from home widowed and orphaned

When a wave packet is incident on a potential barrier

near to the points of my breasts you said on our first date

the electric field is very large

you dance with your hips and feet while I'm all torso

there's a cure for that

as long as it's not the Autenrieth mask

are you nervous?

no that's how I drink my coffee with the stir stick still in it

this is a hard saying they whined to Jesus

and who can understand it?

like when you put both feet into one hole of your coulottes

the body has been my sole means for finding a world

Far from the genitalia where I was born the priest intoned

and stopped having meant peninsula

heart panting hard the irises of your eyes snapped

the event of perception unfolds as reciprocal exchange

what the fuck kind of cross is that?

saliva and wine in the chalice on the altar

yes I take this pear tree

yes you take a forest

so married a certain attitude toward words

it's a Mexican cross a bit tortured

rumor of our coupling rippled

the future pleads for or against us

its profuse blossoms left bud scars crowded around the growing tips

what if the exceptional flowering foretold only a dying off

I took my good shoes from the closet for the interview

brushed off green mold

you were telling me Don't lead with your left foot

just when a solar storm blew out the cell phone

I heard you say Grasshoppers open their spiracles to breathe

take a deep breath with your skin you'll do fine

I got the job I can't say No regrets

on lunch break I drive to Swan Point cemetery

listen to mallards grunt-feeding on roots

their green heads aglow

their specula iridescent blue and listen

to the *hira hira* of little flags flapping in the wind

Dribbling down our steep street

mulberry stains resemble a meteor shower

a wrinkle of gravitational waves passes through

our inquiry is given us whether or not we can speak it

in the world's terms by the world

desire-vein in your neck throbbing

contrails of regret bubble behind us

when truth capitalizes itself

we turn away in profound emotion but

when we look again we see it rewritten in lower case

as you undress for bed your eyes

draw my gaze up from the thighs and belly

as a chimney is said to draw

In English there is no word for the dip of your waist

the inside of your shoe smells like black tea leaves

when densities collide space shudders in response

there are binary stars also locked in mutual thrall

a house finch wipes its beak on the feeder

laughing on the porch drinking seltzer

carbonation burned my nostrils

you are *at night my noon alone*

when I drop the dominant melody

you have left me something to go on

like whisper songs of birds in rain

quartz and alkali feldspars, an intimate graphic intergrowth

veracity confronts us

ravens warning *awe awe*

Through upwelling surges of spontaneity and contingency

menaced by disorder to arrive at a rhythm

the slang naked feelings

arrive at the advent of and then persevere

against the unbreachable

when it splats against matter

light deposits all its energy like moth dust

steelheads rifle ocean currents toward the odor of their natal stream

silver-green scales going blue-black

should you fall

should you hollow inward

wake from dreams worn out and dull as a horse

should you crack and spill the yolk of yourself

you will find in me a stay

and this the promissory note of indebtedness

a proximity that cannot be unhooped

Ligature 2

I'm afraid you have mistaken my intent, I do not say to her. And so we will not speak to each other again.

Small dog barking "like it wants something." But the birds are not singing like they want something.

Early moon, an illuminated fetus.

That deep, intimate smell of a child in sickness, I mean to say: the fusion of fever, skin, hair, and sweat at the neck. But my translation is so slow, my auditors take *child* and *smell* and begin to interject: *the smell of Calomine when he had chicken pox, the smell of the baby's breath after nursing ...*

Requisite tequila shots. The face looking back haggard, lined.

The human ear appears most sensitive to the sound of keening. So that birds seem to vocalize the grief of trees?

A dog on the rooftop, her teats black and long, checks out the boy who walks ahead of us and on the opposite side of the street.

Her come-hither finger curl auditions his response.

As we pass the beggar slouched against the wall with his palm open on his knee, is it still sky of skies or skies of sky?

To watch, in the woman's eyes, the sinking Plimsoll line of her despair.

At the hotel, sunburned and disconsolado, the boy immelmanning across the pool for an hour.

I remember dreaming last night that he loved me.

LATE SUMMER ENTRY

The Landscapes of Sally Mann

Almost all elementary particles have distinct anti-particles.
But the photon serves as its own mirror.

River and Trees

The passage may be so swollen, limpid, and inviting that
it requires considerable effort, a convulsion in seeing's habit, to
encounter the drama. In this composition, to wit, the river
lavishes-out soft tones, rich detail, and gentle, contrasting textures,
but only at first glance. The calm is contradictory. For when we
find the river *holding still*—in imitation of itself—it barely
impresses a likeness.

The depicted instant: a galvanic pre-storm eclipse.
On a bridge, the photographer bends, shrouded behind her tripod.
As she guesses the exposure time, lightning hisses and rips so close
that the air, for seconds, isn't breathable. At once, the river
quicksilvers. Its surface bulks and brightens. The heft of the
scene, though, and the dynamic tension flee to the margins.
There,

in the rumpled quiet of the trees, we catch the most
animate qualities. In the riffle of leafy detail, we sense the
respiration of the forest.

And while we absorb this disturbance in a merely apparent
repose, our stomach rolls—as when an elevator begins to descend.
We detect in the blurred trees a peristaltic contraction. We feel
the landscape giving birth to our vision.

Photo Canto

As its allure clamors

    from the corners, swarming,

  preparatory, we imagine

ourselves into the scene where a river

  irradiates its forest.

    Brush, sedge,

and branches blend,

   their outlines illegible,

      as though flayed

  by the frenzy of a day

    that thrashed itself out

among light-eating leaves. Now

sullen fog

   shutters the eye. The rock

      dissolves into glint,

  a blot of cryptic menace,

and shadows

   condense into a living blackness

where non-being stirs, where the swirl

of unborn things,

    like a nursery of spiders,

stirs beyond our senses.

Ghost Sonata

The fulcrum of the composition is the sheared off, gnarly trunk. In contradiction of death's irreversibility, it has burst into leaf. It leans forward, toward us, producing an effect similar to the entasis or swelling of a classical pillar. Isolation magnifies its solemnity. Beyond the trunk, the horizon lists. On one side, foliage goes fuzzy, while on the other side, a strange flare burns.

Strain between focal points is sustained by the central figure of the ruptured tree. Mute, but implicative. A leafy explosion crowns the severed totem. So at the border between a tangible and an intangible world, life climbs onto death's shoulders.

Road and Tree

Lucent road, first letter.   Evening spooked with light.

Quarter moon road   with the darkness inside it, and full moon

sky with the tree inside it.   Curved road in the gloaming.

Oak trunk, a vector of force   punched upward. Held in place

by the stenciled circle of light. Lit   road bearing a trunk of its own

darkness. Circle of light split   like a cat's eye. Road

curling left, eye   cutting right. Barely there in the soft

dirt, footprints and dogprints   commingling in the throat

of the road where voices,   also, have fallen with pollen.

This is an inner landscape, for even   as light came back like bees

to the camera proclaiming   the photograph, the place

altered, never availed   itself at all. A hem of cirrus

brushed the sun, the Carolina wren's   *cheery* gave way

to a full moon   in the afternoon and little grass frogs.

Dry puffballs detonated   into a cloud of gold spores as a hoof

lifted, and even if it had pictured   a real terrain for

one moment, of what place   is it a memory now?

The image strands itself, a word   knocked loose

from the language, a tooth   under a pillow.

And the place itself was neither   fully read nor erased since it never

ceased being written. Only   a word was pronounced, only

the instrument   clicked.

Science & Steepleflower

The temperate, velvet sheen on the water is not applied, but
constitutive. Just the stream utters light. The woods are hushed.
The vagueness of a near shoreline endows the water with a
transfigured, opalescent lour. We see the reflection of trees, partly
erased in splotches, as through a delicate mist. Our eyes following
the stream until shadows pinch off the flow of our gaze.

Because the realm is uncertain, it prompts us. Not placid,
but haunting, this pastoral. The shaggy forest is dim, private,
oneiric. And the circular frame of the image closes inward.
Called *vignetting*, this girdling dark is a metaphor, and it has two
meanings. It signals the onset of our blink, and as such, can be
read as a sign of the evanescence of the image that, even in the act
of preservation, must be relinquished. However it is equally
indicative of the incipient vision opening to us from the other side
of consciousness, the muscular curtain drawing back from the
beginning of dream.

Collodion

Dogwood, laurel, rhododendron,   Judas tree. Traveling

to places they had seen   in magazines, tourists

found the original   less authentic

than the impression   with which they came.

The more intense the emotion, the slower   the speed.

Incarnate and carbonized,   the photograph gives evidence

of an arousal to be had   in no other form.

The hedge, not visible,   I feel it

and know it.   A *dark cloud,* wrote a monk,

illuminates the night. Oh,   aperture revealing

the divine gesture   as a pure demonstration of the world:

guide me back from   interpretation to sensation to

vision, for one   stroke of a wet cloth

may wipe the picture   out.

Ivy Brick Wall

It never aims to create an illusion of reality. Instead, the warped lens allows for a new set of relationships behind swirling frets. The wall confronts a flotsam of vortical energy and tree limbs transparentize in the blast.

Enmeshed in a field of concentric force, the spectator is drawn toward a wormhole of brightness, not depth but another dimension entire. A light which is life source.

It is this originary force that transforms the ordinary into the exultant. Here, where light authors act and meaning, where whelming ivy overwrites brickwork.

The nucleus of the image is all verb, the seen availing itself to our seeing. When there are no stable terms, there are no faithful things.

Argosy for Rock and Grass

A snapping turtle, its saw-tooth   tail and keeled shell

nesting in the river mud,   blows water

through its nostrils   until the surface froths.

Wind   runs through the distant

assembly of pin oaks: a family graveyard, untended

in bracken fern. Five   concrete headstones

decorated with marbles   Child, Child, Child, Child, Child.

The landscape clutches   its long roots, its concealed

life animates   the loam. A drawn-out exposure

nets traces of movement—   flying birds, trembling leaves

leaven thought. Glinting in rock: mica, feldspar, cyanide.

Although place is depicted, no   sign in the world

corresponds to this   image. There is no source

outside itself   for such radiance. Stone

pulls at grass and   the treeline wavers

like something proposed   and forgotten.

But to fault   the image for its lack

of correlative, we would   miss its fullness

coming to be.   The river is named

The Holy Ghost. We believe   what we do not know.

Bridge & Swimmer

Our eye goes past the hieroglyphic tree to the swimmer
carving a wake in the water. And almost to the railroad bridge
from which the swimmer might have dived. Then, as though
come to the end of its tether,
our gaze returns, pulling toward the blemish
on the surface of the print. An L-shaped chemical dribble,
it sabotages the scene's transparence
and siphons off its easy appeal.

At the same time, the blemish
joins together the realms
of seer and swimmer
in our experience of plunging
into and out of the image.

The Broken Tower

Outside the fever of faces, there is this place
along Purgatory Creek, past the grist mill's

                           stone ruin, a road
pulled from darkness and stretched out to dry
in mute morning air. The scene's complexity,
its shifting depths,

                 derive from an interplay
of directed tensions—the rearing trees
and tower, the prone ditch and road. We
waver between chords of symmetry, unable

                   to pin down the beat.
Of all we survey, how often are we
distracted by the least substantial—the ditch
gaping like a grave for the tower,
catfish heads scattered in the dirt, and

                  ditchwater dull as resin.
Meanwhile, saturated by the density
of light, the tower and trees blend
into a compassion

           where all the sight lines meet.

Late Summer Entry

Brush-hogged here last week, beckons.

Dog won't sit on the stubble, beckons.

Distant peak, Cambrian quartzite beckons.

Dipping northwest, beckons.

They mine corundum here, beckons.

Grinds her plates with corundum, beckons.

Can you smell collodion, beckons.

Ether and alcohol, cold as an eel, beckons.

Blackening her fingertips, beckons.

Stiffens into membrane, beckons.

Shoot collodion in the full sun, beckons.

So so fragile, beckons.

Pours it onto the plate, beckons.

Three minutes to climb the hill, three minutes to shoot it, beckons.

Under a cape, composing an upside-down image, beckons.

Felt Rider hat in one hand, plate in the other, beckons.

Fingers the lens, beckons.

Pulls out the block, beckons.

The camera quivers, beckons.

Can you photograph a Carolina wren's song, beckons.

The collodion fills with birdsong, beckons.

With the scent of ripening pawpaws, beckons.

From the pawpaw tree behind her, beckons.

Extracts the glass plate, beckons.

Walks back to the truck, beckons.

Over the stiff stubble, the dog following, beckons.

Pulls out the chemical tray, beckons.

The spring-driven trap, thwarting light, beckons.

Click, beckons.

The plate sinks into the tray, beckons.

Gently the dark blows in, beckons.

So figure passes into shadow.

Ligature 3

One hairy woodpecker follows another around the trunk.

Word as sap, I scrawled. As soon as possible.

Waiting for the boy, a gangly pup lolls at the edge of the plaza. Rolls onto its back, attacks a scrap of napkin.

From our table, I watch the woman's eyes shuffle the faces of passersby. Her earrings have stretched the holes in her lobes into suggestive slits.

When we first met, the words we whispered were erotic. Later it was the silence.

A stranger asks me to accompany her son to the men's room. He has an eagerness to pees, she translates.

Humility is pride's strictest flourish, its grass script. But to submit to the world is integration, the beginning of—

The boy picks a leaf to lay beside the rhinoceros beetle flailing on its back. The beetle rights itself against the leaf. Meanwhile the twig begins to bleed.

All the while we sit jostled against each other on the crowded bus, angry and unspeaking, an electrostatic charge joins the fine hairs of our legs.

When he doesn't come home, I search for him. Under the streetlamp, a dust-colored scorpion, hatchlings riding her, raises her pedipalps.

Haunted town. In the predawn, muffled breakers. Roosters. A cat slowly eases itself into a garbage can.

Without language, appearance still asks questions of itself.

He has been photographing pariah dogs. You must be inside pain to feel it.

I wake to hear a woman outside the window pishing warblers.

The boy points out to me a cartography of snail tracks on a broad avocado leaf.

Not the sentence is for the words but the words are for the sentence. Two of us withdraw to make room for the third.

A parrot walks from the table onto the boy's outstretched hand. He picks it up before he sees the half of its wing shorn cleanly as with a scissor.

MISSION THIEF

Mission Thief

Picking up toward evening
      bay breezes quicken
      the Mission and
      fuchsia petals plop
      onto slabs of root-tilted sidewalk
      a local tectonics we maneuver
      you and I fecund with our
      renewed vows en route
      to La Cumbre with its Aztec
      mural and gorditos
      at the curb, windows opaque,
      a black '75 Cadillac
      rocks high up and drops
      back on pneumatic shocks
      a whiff of carne asada
      poles mummified with posters:
      Has Visto Este Niño / Thrash Polka at Slims—
      while

                              five blocks away
the imminent lays its egg
in the eye of evening and
what begins as tenderness
will end at Calvary
for whose devotion can I claim
to aim wholly at you if holding
your hand even so
my eyes swivel
to see the figure at the door
with dim desire or is it
nostalgia finally, mere registration,
an animal impulse
tightens the plexus—
only at the crossing only
through horizons—
three blocks away
a white-haired man
the collar of his jacket
stained with sweat
closes his saddlebags and leans
his bicycle, all he owns,
against the pharmacy wall
while a panhandler puts down
his bagged bottle
by the lightpost and watches

you reach for

my hand as we cross Dolores I spit

sidewise into my shadow

when you aren't looking

the monitor on a stool outside the Mission Revival

plays a live feed

of the sermon within

a bleak scene few men

one child about twelve

sweaty preacher's sthenic rant

dressed well

a parishioner slips out

through front doors but before

they close, another—one

of us, the assembly of voyeurs—

ushers herself in:

so water evaporating from treetops

siphons water through leaf

which siphons water

through xylem up the trunk

from roots maybe when

one escapes

another is sucked inside

who will rescue her?

not me and not open-mouthed

opportunity

eyeing the bike against the wall

we do not see

the man the panhandler steal the bike

though others can

two sparrows titter in fescue

on the traffic island

we continue to stroll

in urban intimacy the same

tuned rhythm our synced steps

mark us a couple

a couplet on the page of scrawled noise

men sawing pavement at the corner

thick rap bass thumping

from open cars a Harley

growls around Guerrero

Mexican songs at the café we pass

a splash of Mandarin washes over

the protected pool of our taking-it-in

only at the crossing only through horizons

with roses for sale, approaching the pair

eating at a curbside table,

an ink-haired Guatemalan girl in a red dress

her shyness hovers at the edge of their plates like a fly

the bicycle thief wobbles our way

long strips of stratus make it

a dropjaw sunset I stumble and

from behind you

catch the swing phase of your walk

erotic your left foot pigeon-toed

hips narrow as a boy's

but what hatched in the alley and left

that urine stink and sparrows

thikke as motes in the sonne-beem

and two starlings

their wings scissored behind them

like mournful rabbis

I used to imagine strangers naked

you say now I imagine them in coffins

the back of our hands touch

you squeeze my thumb the body

ambiguously subject and

object a dog tied to a fireplug sneezes

the man passing by says Bless you

a little sordid and still warm leftover

flan-yellow of day remains

before what was once called civil-dark

when it grew too dim to work and

the ice man with his iron-scorpion

dragged to a kitchen his last block

already the future is cued up and closing in

summoning us to what?

the thief peddles toward us

though we have not seen him

when you turn

your face to ask me if

Mexicans call hummingbirds colibrí

or chupaflor flower-sucker the light

reveals your irises' steel rims

dark hoops that hold the blue in

and do we invent this privacy

the privilege to brim with each other

as though our rillet might be

deducted from the mainstream

as if we were stirred together

past mere propinquity

and the desperate and enraged

were eased by such a day

as in that story of the wolf

unstalking its prey the familiar

rapture I presume you feel

with me even as I tongue

the prickles in my throat

that foretell a cold and step back

to the brink

of thee, smudged

      newspaper print where your

      fingers brushed your nose

      at once we sense commotion ahead

      as faces one by one like cards

      when a bet is called

      flip their open expression

      toward us

      what is happening

      hurtles our way in shouts shouts

      as if something were

      being birthed, alert

      I see the man on bicycle

      under a neon taqueria sign—

      only at the crossing only through

      horizons between—someone yells

      something inarticulate

      almost to us

                              he is racing

recklessly up the sidewalk—startled

pedestrians jump aside—

already plummeting

from prospective to present

his counterpoint

divorcing you from me

from the rhythm of our tangency

our breaking into *my* and *my*

I lurch and cannot feel yet and fail to rise

into the revision

of circumstance as though

I tumbled from stairs

to a spot-lit stage where you were

cut off from me by the light

a sidewalk of strangers

severed from concerns that seconds prior

perfectly contained them

waylaid and yielding their leads

for the role of audience

the drama hurrying on its way

the head of event expanding

the dark head of event crowning before us

and it still is not clear

      what is happening what

      is impinging on us

      an obligation I hear

      an indecipherable whinny of alarm

      the immediate stamping in its stall

      as the thief nears our end of the block

      as light that left a galaxy

      in the Hercules cluster

      600 million years ago

      now burns through the horizon

      and ignites a life

      that was never beyond my seeing

      and the same wakes up from itself

      pain of the eye overwhelmed by light

      while I strain for clues

      in the surprised faces

      the many misconstrued bodies

      off balance on pause

      to isolate the bicyclist

      in his singular tumult

      he who supplants you

      who makes his claim

      greater on me

      he himself custodian now

      of this present in which

      against inertia I strain to act

      but

                    how quickly he penetrates

the blister of my regard

from which you've been extracted

as the world goes quiet

and the event of identification

gathers me into its theme

handlebar and rear-rack panniers

swinging side to side half

standing on pedals whose

wild joggling wide-wet eyes urge

No no don't stop me

I mean to grab for his arm

but your hand stays mine and

from an infinite distance

I recall you

your presence

blows in, a red petal,

three of us

briefly enjoined

pooling our volitions

you tug my shirt

my hand slaps his neck

half-assed scuffle my

knuckles scrape the stucco wall

as he flails

      at me I hear but

      whom do I hear?

      my failure all along to

      secern even you

      who are saying *No*

      the word rings and through the ring

      a thin scarf of disapproval

      draws across my vague intent

      awkward in the struggle

      to hold him to judge what

      effort to make with whom

      am I thrashing

      a bent stalk a question mark

      for a backbone

      my hand touching his shoulder

      so tentative and slow

      the gesture might be taken

      for an act of deputation

      a surplus of devotion the

      bestowal of meaning then

      he stiff-arms me and

      I turn

like the other

spectators, a pure stare

now a singularity uncoupled once again

that readily from you like the dissolving glow

of a clicked-off light

the floater behind a closed eye

and so combined elements

on the stalk of an instant

unpetal their parts in wind

a hand bleeding a man on bicycle

a murky sense of restraint which is you

breached from the *we* I presupposed

lifted from the felt

background and placed here again

near but across the caesura

the rent stanza in our accord

as what I am cracks

into two acts

and one replays the scene

revising it toward

some imagined salvific end

if trajectory

is divisible

I gauge the thief's increasing

distance from me

instinctively as when flying

I measure the gap

from jet to ground

with an image of my body falling

a red petal

he veers to the street

and something summons me again

a wheeze spins me around

to see a white-haired man

in a sluggish run

slather of mucus under

pigeon-hole nostrils, his gaze

nailed ahead *at the crossing*

my eyes put on his face

his mouth a gasping rictus

as he plods past

never to catch

what

                    lulled on routine and self

and casual neglect I let slip

rooted in place around me

a block of storefronts and trees

a man on foot falling farther behind

the one on bike

the rest of us unrescued

stopped in time transfixed

to this stark spectacle of our separateness

making its stand

hammering its horizons home

behind which each of us says I don't know

who you are

you never broke through me

the key makes no sound

when you go to play

the world shifts

along a hairline crack

you can't tell

what is happening

until it moves on and is gone

as someone and someone's grief

careen around a corner

Ligature 4

The bioluminescent undersides of squid render them invisible to predators below. That the radiance of the boy's anger might protect him.

Walking the dog and stepping on a patch of repaired road, I remember the soft spot in his head.

You're deaf as a beagle. No, you are.

Can I feel the tide's drag on the turning earth increase each day's duration?

A hair in my nostril has gone white.

In absolute night, from my bed, I hear him aiming for the toilet's center. The sound deepens, voice finding its register.

Scientists call it an entangled system.

We survive Christmas, his face pressed to the smooshed bosom of his grandmother in a house so immaculate, the spider in the seam of the ceiling stands out obscenely.

Like a star at the outskirts of the galaxy, and slung around by the gravity of dark matter. For now, he goes where we go, but he does not belong to us.

I begin to begin my sentences leaning toward him, taking a deep breath.

He relinquishes the conversation with a contraction of his pupils.

What is for one of us the throb of the immediate is, for the other, the imminent mundane.

When napalm hits my brain, he takes on the tranquillity of a blinking newt.

She finds a photograph of him at seven. The sheer *expressed* of his face. As among Michelangelo's early drawings, there is a copy of Masacchio's lost *Sagra*, the consecration.

We search our memories of him for a certain unity of characteristics that would hold through the permutations he now submits to us.

When it clings to the wire-and-rug surrogate, lab technicians shock it again. Instead of releasing, it clings tighter.

Throwing himself into the back seat after wrestling practice, mat burns on his cheek and forehead.

His muteness an onomatopoeia of the rising moon.